CHRISTMAS FUN

A SPOT-IT CHALLENGE

by Jennifer L. Marks

Capstone press

Mankato, Minnesota

A+ books

A+ Books are published by Capstone Press,
151 Good Counsel Drive, P.O. Box 669, Mankato, Minnesota 56002.
www.capstonepress.com

1 2 3 4 5 6 14 13 12 11 10 09

Library of Congress Cataloging-in-Publication Data
Marks, Jennifer L.
    Christmas fun : a spot-it challenge / by Jennifer L. Marks.
    p. cm. — (A+ books. Spot it)
    Includes bibliographical references.
    Summary: "Simple text invites the reader to find items hidden in Christmas-themed
photographs" — Provided by publisher.
    ISBN-13: 978-1-4296-2219-6 (library binding)
    ISBN-10: 1-4296-2219-9 (library binding)
    1. Christmas — Juvenile literature. I. Title. II. Series.
GT4985.5.M265 2009
394.2663 — dc22   2008045470

Credits

Juliette Peters, set designer
All photos by Capstone Press Photo Studio

Note to Parents, Teachers, and Librarians
Spot It is an interactive series that supports literacy development and reading enjoyment. Readers
utilize visual discrimination skills to find objects among fun-to-peruse photographs with busy
backgrounds. Readers also build vocabulary through thematic groupings, develop visual memory
ability through repeated readings, and improve strategic and associative thinking skills by
experimenting with different visual search methods.

The author dedicates this book to her sister Rachel, who begins her countdown to Christmas
in August.

Table of Contents

Snow Folk Gathering

Can you spot...

- a woodland gnome?
- a green fish?
- a bumblebee?
- a button cap?
- a bathroom sink?
- a broom?

A Doggone Christmas

Can you spot...

- a naughty squirrel?
- a basket of yarn?
- a cowboy boot?
- a pliers?
- a wire whisk?
- a red teacup?

X-Mess Decorations

Can you spot...

- a rubber chicken?
- a toilet seat?
- a cement mixer?
- a wooden train?
- a real hot dog?
- a faceless friend?
- a yellow wrench?

Gift Wrap Madness

Can you spot...

- a bone?
- a blue watch?
- a baseball?
- a bowling pin?
- a pencil sharpener?
- a pair of binoculars?

Ding-a-Ling, Bells Ring

Can you spot...

- a silver car?
- two tiny trumpets?
- a nickel?
- a musical tie?
- a fishing hook?
- a Slinky?
- an eraser?
- a fire chief's badge?

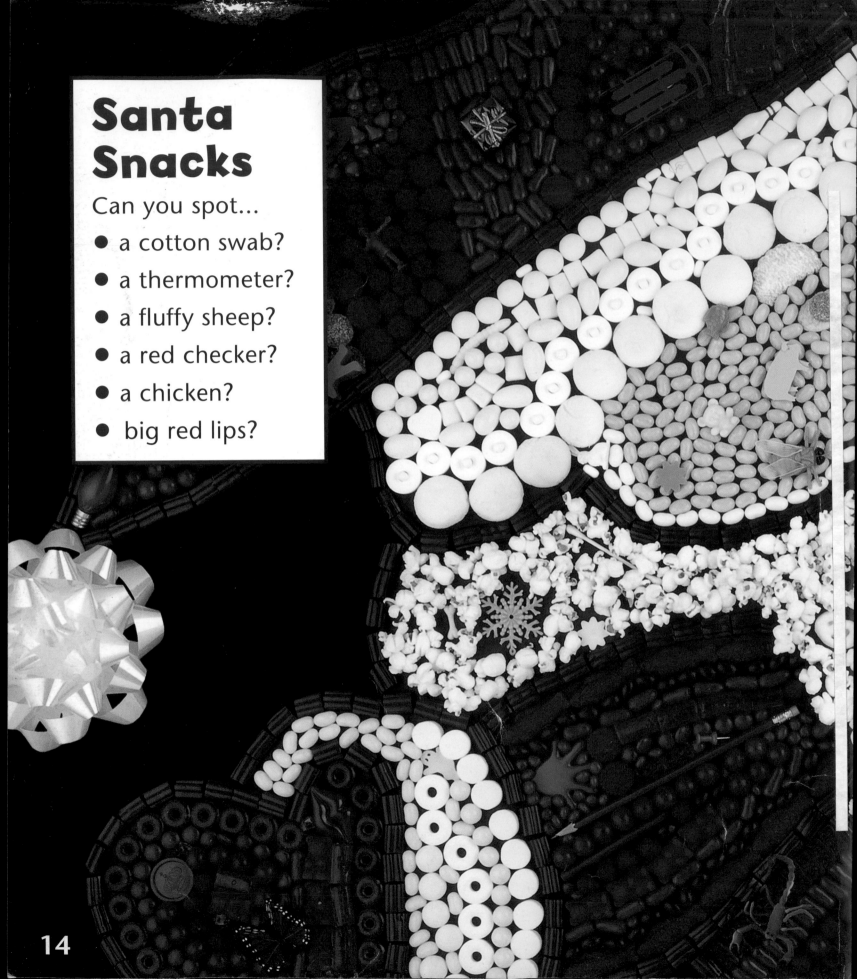

Santa Snacks

Can you spot...

- a cotton swab?
- a thermometer?
- a fluffy sheep?
- a red checker?
- a chicken?
- big red lips?

14

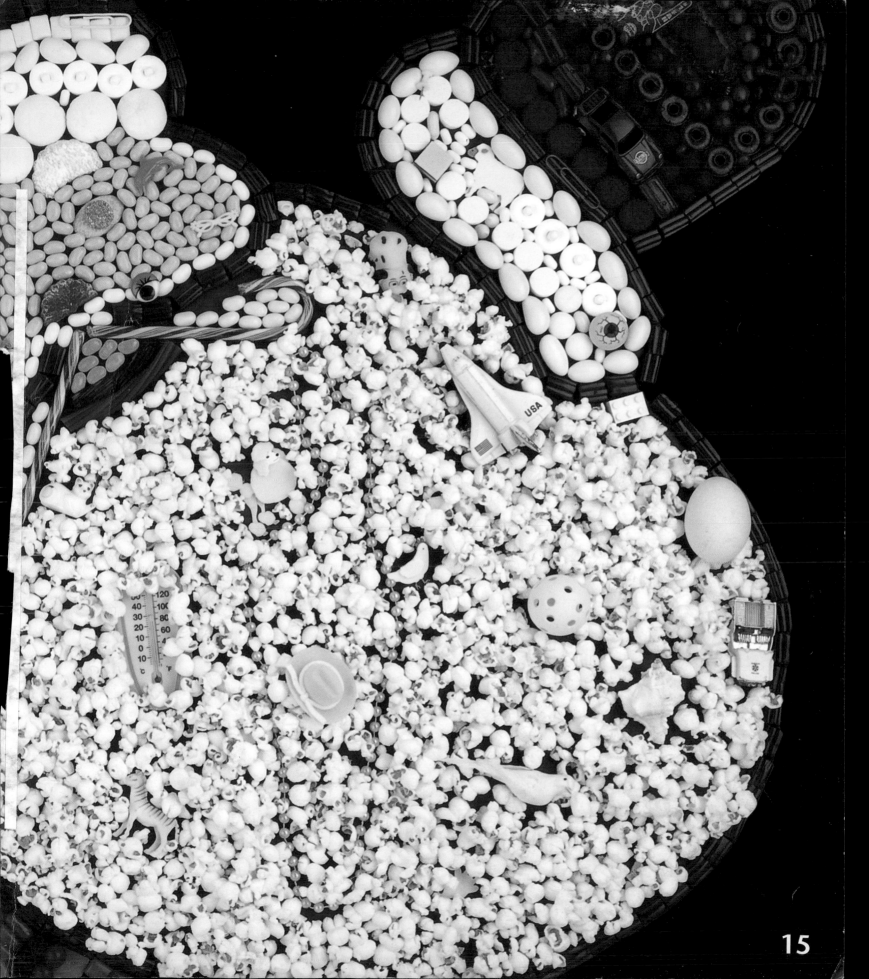

A Tropical Christmas

Can you spot...

- Santa Claus?
- an eye patch?
- a fire hydrant?
- a paddle?
- a treasure chest?
- a sailboat?
- a tiny angel?

Beastly Christmas Feast

Can you spot...

- a pink flamingo?
- a ketchup bottle?
- two artichokes?
- a red bathtub?
- a fire truck?
- a red mushroom?
- a number 1?

Gingerbread Village

Can you spot...

- four lost mittens?
- a camel?
- a cowboy?
- a globe?
- a snorkel?
- a headless horseman?
- a pinecone?

Toys for Christmas

Can you spot...

- a seashell?
- a fork?
- an apple?
- a merry-go-round?
- a blue letter J?
- an ice cream scoop?

Blue, Blue Christmas

Can you spot...

- a spotted toad?
- a paper clip?
- some cool shades?
- two elephants?
- a football helmet?
- a toothbrush?
- a dinosaur?

24

Cookies Galore

Can you spot...

- a tree frog?
- a clothespin?
- a star cookie cutter?
- a wrench?
- a turtle?
- tiny cookies on a mini plate?

Spot Even More!

Snow Folk Gathering 4

Try to find a hiker, a fire hydrant, a toilet, a cone, a tiny rake, a green paper clip, and a piece of candy corn.

A Doggone Christmas 6

See if you can spot a cake, a mouse, a carrot, a mouse trap, a hot dog, a leaf, and a big shoe.

X-Mess Decorations 8

Take another look and find an airplane, a soldier, a ship, a sandwich, a blue house fly, and a fishing fish.

Gift Wrap Madness 10

Now find a ladybug, a shiny pickle, fuzzy dice, a sea horse, two dinosaurs, and a winner's trophy.

Ding-a-Ling, Bells Ring 12

Now spot a strawberry, five Christmas stockings, a nail clipper, and two bell-shaped cookie cutters.

Santa Snacks 14

Try to spy some glasses, a dove, a number 1 fan hand, a sled, a scorpion, an egg, and a jeep.

A Tropical Christmas 16

See if you can find a skeleton, red Christmas bells, an octopus, a chair, and a pair of earmuffs.

Beastly Christmas Feast 18

Try to find a cowboy hat, a butterfly, a mitten, a roll of toilet paper, white shoelaces, and a soccer ball.

Gingerbread Village 20

Now spot a gumball machine, a green monster, a bunny with a carrot, a teddy bear, and Santa Claus.

Toys for Christmas 22

Try to find a green colored pencil, an airplane, a sheriff's star, a banana, and a sandcastle.

Blue, Blue Christmas 24

Now look for a tiny blue car, two silver stars, a sea horse, a sparkly white pear, and two butterflies.

Cookies Galore 26

Take one last look and find a red "A," a yellow button, a comb, Santa's boots, a pink shoe, and a silver bell.

Extreme Spot-It Challenge

Just can't get enough Spot-It action? Find the items in this extra Christmas challenge.

- ticket booth
- taxi
- officer's badge
- spoon
- the ace of spades
- skateboard
- black shoe
- penny
- white dove
- two blue trees
- drinking straw
- two gingerbread cookie cutters
- ear of corn
- battery
- bar of soap
- green snake
- wooden match

Read More

Kidslabel. *Spot 7 Christmas.* Spot 7. San Francisco: Chronicle, 2006.

Marks, Jennifer L. *Fun and Games: A Spot-It Challenge.* Spot It. Mankato, Minn.: Capstone Press, 2009.

Marzollo, Jean. *I Spy Santa Claus.* Scholastic Reader. New York: Scholastic, 2005.

Internet Sites

FactHound offers a safe, fun way to find educator-approved Internet sites related to this book.

Here's what you do:
1. Visit *www.facthound.com*
2. Choose your grade level.
3. Begin your search.

This book's ID number is 9781429622196.

FactHound will fetch the best sites for you!